j623.74    Simons, Lisa M. B.,
SIM         1969-

           The kids' guide to
            military vehicles.

$25.32

| DATE | | |
|---|---|---|
| | | |
| | | |
| | | |
| | | |
| | | |
| | | |
| | | |
| | | |
| | | |
| | | |
| | | |
| | | |
| | | |
| | | |

STAINS PG 17 & INSIDE    BACK COVER 4/22/14 PC

EDGE BOOKS™

# The Kids' Guide to

# Military VEHICLES

### by Lisa M. Bolt Simons

**Consultant:**

Raymond L. Puffer, PhD
Historian, Ret.
Edwards Air Force Base History Office

Capstone press®

Mankato, Minnesota

Books published by Capstone Press are manufactured with paper
containing at least 10 percent post-consumer waste.

*Library of Congress Cataloging-in-Publication Data*
Simons, Lisa M. B., 1969–
The kids' guide to military vehicles / by Lisa M. Bolt Simons.
   p. cm. — (Edge books. Kids' guides)
   Includes bibliographical references and index.
   Summary: "Describes a wide range of military vehicles, including wheeled and
tracked vehicles, ships, airplanes, and unmanned vehicles" — Provided by publisher.
   ISBN 978-1-4296-3370-3 (library binding)
   1. Vehicles, Military — Juvenile literature. 2. Airplanes, Military — Juvenile literature.
3. Warships — Juvenile literature. 4. Vehicles, Remotely piloted — Juvenile literature.
I. Title. II. Series.
UG615.S56 2010
623.7'4 — dc22
                                                                    2009010958

**Editorial Credits**

Gillia Olson, editor; Veronica Bianchini, designer; Jo Miller, media researcher

**Photo Credits**

AP Images/Bob Child, 24
DEFENSEIMAGERY.MIL/Christopher J. Varville, DOD Civ, 18 (bottom); John Byerly, 8 (top);
   LCPL Patrick Green, USMC, 29 (middle); TSGT Mike Buytas, USAF, 11 (bottom); TSGT
   Russell E. Cooley IV, USAF, 5 (top)
DoD photo/Navy Lt. Peter Scheu, 16
iStockphoto/Jared DeCinque, cover (Howitzer)
Shutterstock/Neale Cousland, cover (background gear detail); ozgur artug, cover (camouflage
   background)
U.S. Air Force photo, 12 (left), 13 (middle), 14–15, 15 (bottom); Master Sgt. Andy Dunaway, cover
   (F-16), 12 (right), 15 (top); Senior Airman Julianne Showalter, 29 (bottom); Senior Airman
   Michael Frye, 13 (top); Senior Airman Steve Czyz, 9; Staff Sgt. DeNoris A. Mickle, 10; Staff Sgt.
   Joe Laws, 8 (bottom); Tech. Sgt. Erik Gudmundson, 17; Tech. Sgt. Sabrina Johnson, 29 (top)
U.S. Army photo by Spc. Luke Thornberry, 7 (inset)
U.S. Coast Guard photo by PA2 Nyxolyno Cangemi, 23 (inset)
U.S. Marine Corps photo by Cpl. James F. Cline III, 4; Sgt. Ezekiel R. Kitandwe, 19 (bottom);
   Sgt. Jason W. Fudge, cover (MRAP), 11 (top)
U.S. Navy Illustration courtesy Northrop Grumman Newport News Shipbuilding, 20–21
U.S. Navy Photo by MC1 David McKee, 28; MC2 Brandon A. Teeples, 26; MC2 James R. Evans,
   13 (bottom), 18 (top); MC2 Jason R. Zalasky, 5 (bottom); MC2 Kimberly Clifford, 25; MC2
   Richard Doolin, 19 (top); MC3 Geoffrey Lewis, 22–23; MC3 Michael Starkey, 27 (bottom); Paul
   Farley, cover (frigate); PH1 Ted Banks, 6–7; PH2 Prince A. Hughes III, 27 (top)

# TABLE OF CONTENTS

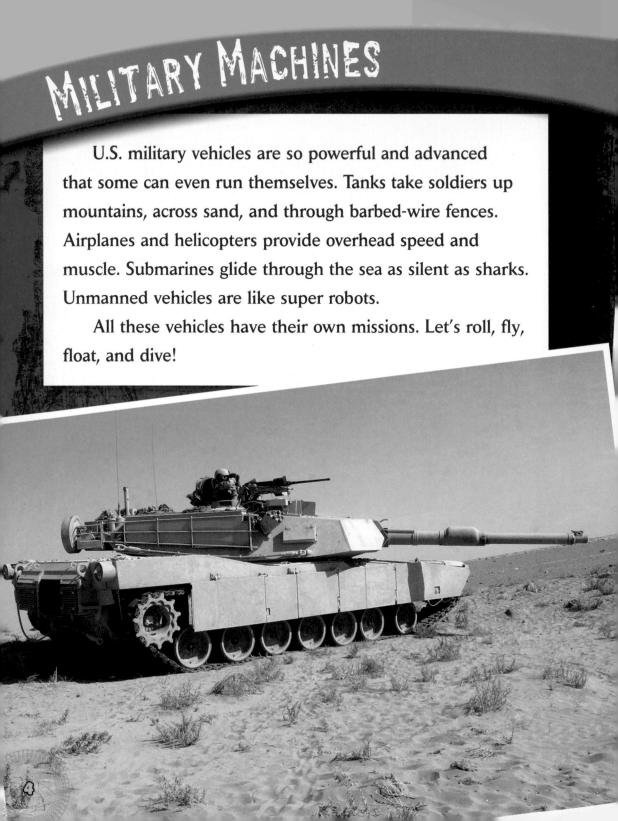

# MILITARY MACHINES

U.S. military vehicles are so powerful and advanced that some can even run themselves. Tanks take soldiers up mountains, across sand, and through barbed-wire fences. Airplanes and helicopters provide overhead speed and muscle. Submarines glide through the sea as silent as sharks. Unmanned vehicles are like super robots.

All these vehicles have their own missions. Let's roll, fly, float, and dive!

## Fun Fact:

The U.S. military has more than 1.1 million active troops and at least as many reserve troops.

It's the tank's job to search for and destroy enemies. The military uses these big bullies to strike fear into the enemy. They also keep crews safe with their heavy armor. Three Abrams tank variations are in use today. They are the M1, M1A1, and M1A2. Soldiers call the Abrams "The Beast" and "Dracula."

## M1A1 ABRAMS

The M2 machine gun takes out targets with light armor.

The 120-millimeter main gun launches a variety of rounds. The range is about 2 miles (3.2 kilometers).

The track runs on seven road wheels on each side. The track is about 2 feet (.6 meter) wide.

## THE CREW

The Abrams has a crew of four. The tank commander directs the mission. The driver steers the tank. The gunner finds targets and fires the main gun and two machine guns. The loader keeps weapons loaded and fires another machine gun.

Crew members can sit in the turret. The main gun is also mounted on the turret.

The drive wheel on each side is powered by the engine. The drive wheel moves the whole track.

Other tracked vehicles may look like tanks, but don't be fooled. All of them have armor, but their missions are different.

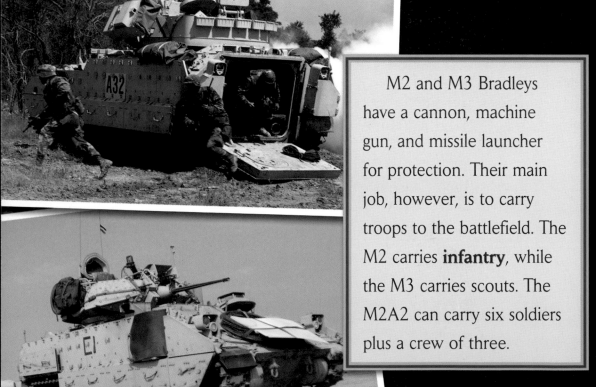

M2 and M3 Bradleys have a cannon, machine gun, and missile launcher for protection. Their main job, however, is to carry troops to the battlefield. The M2 carries **infantry**, while the M3 carries scouts. The M2A2 can carry six soldiers plus a crew of three.

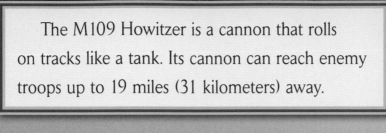

The M109 Howitzer is a cannon that rolls on tracks like a tank. Its cannon can reach enemy troops up to 19 miles (31 kilometers) away.

**infantry** — members of the military trained to fight on land

Sometimes troops need wheels, not tracks. Wheeled vehicles are usually faster and cheaper to maintain than tracked vehicles.

The High Mobility Multipurpose Wheeled Vehicle (HMMWV) is nicknamed the Humvee. It replaced the jeep in the mid-1980s as an all-purpose vehicle. Humvees carry weapons and troops. They are also used as ambulances. Armored Humvees with large guns act as bodyguards for other trucks.

The military created Mine Resistant Ambush Protected (MRAP) vehicles to hold up better against small explosives than the Humvee. There are several designs, including the Cougar, Buffalo, and MaxxPro.

Cougar

The Stryker is a Light Armored Vehicle (LAV). One kind carries infantry. The other has a cannon. This eight-wheeled vehicle is quiet and safe. If you're riding in a tank and the track comes off, you stop. On a Stryker, you can keep moving even if all four tires on one side are flat.

## Fun Fact:

In the 2007 movie *Transformers*, the Decepticon named Bonecrusher was modeled after a Buffalo MRAP.

# FIGHTER JETS AND BOMBERS

Fighter jets rocket into the air faster than you can say "speed of sound." Fighters are designed to shoot down enemy planes, but they also carry bombs for ground targets.

The F-22 Raptor, the newest jet, flies up to **Mach** 2. Its shape, paint, and internal weapons make it difficult to see on radar.

The F-16 Fighting Falcon is a lightweight, nimble fighter. It's better than most planes at withstanding the forces that put stress on planes during high-speed turns, lifts, or dives.

**Mach** — a unit of measurement for speeds faster than the speed of sound; Mach 2 is twice the speed of sound.

# DEMONSTRATION TEAMS

The U.S. Navy Blue Angels and the U.S. Air Force Thunderbirds are demonstration teams. They perform fighter jet moves at shows around the world. If these jets are called to battle, they are painted with standard colors and loaded with weapons within 72 hours.

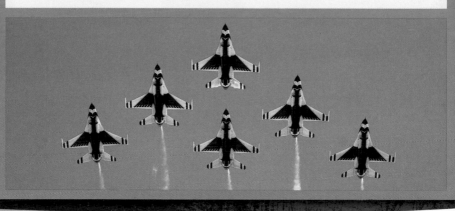

A weapons officer (WO) makes the F-15E Strike Eagle unique. The WO sits in a rear cockpit and selects targets as the pilot flies.

Bombs, missiles, and a cannon arm the Navy's F/A-18 Hornet. The newest one is the Super Hornet. It flies farther and has better radar than the original Hornet.

Bombers are heavy hitters designed to destroy ground targets. They can hit anything, anywhere, at any time.

The B-52 Stratofortress can launch or drop the greatest variety of weapons. The enemy can't even hide in bunkers with thick walls. Bombs called "bunker busters" burst through concrete walls before exploding.

payload — the total weight of items carried by an airplane

nuclear — having to do with the energy created by splitting atoms; this energy can be used to make extremely powerful weapons or as a power source.

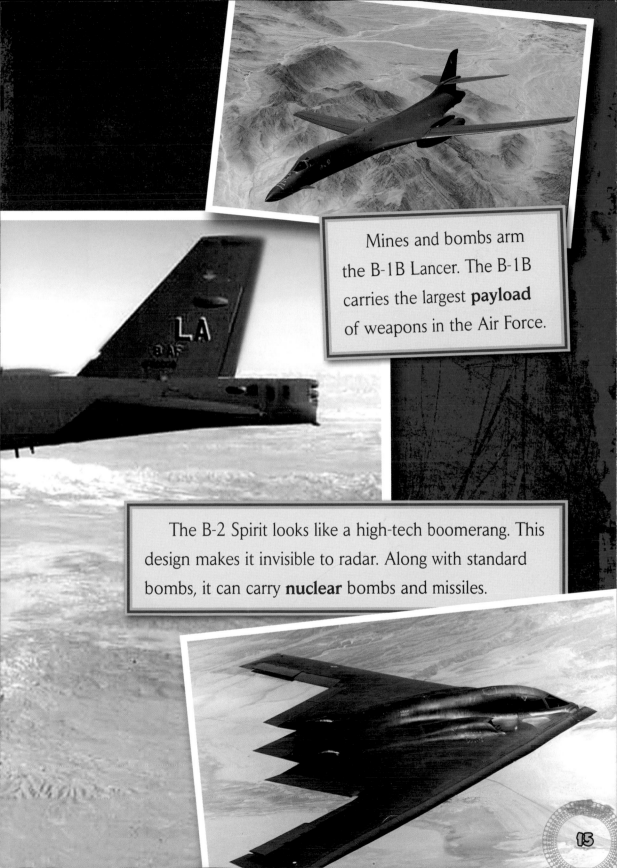

Mines and bombs arm the B-1B Lancer. The B-1B carries the largest **payload** of weapons in the Air Force.

The B-2 Spirit looks like a high-tech boomerang. This design makes it invisible to radar. Along with standard bombs, it can carry **nuclear** bombs and missiles.

# Cargo Planes

Cargo planes look like supersized passenger planes. They may carry passengers – nearly 130 fully armed soldiers – or act as flying gas stations.

A KC-10 Extender refuels an F/A-18 Hornet.

The main mission of the KC-135 Stratotanker and KC-10 Extender is to refuel planes in the air. The KC-135 carries 200,000 pounds (90,700 kilograms) of fuel. The newer KC-10 carries almost two times more.

C-130s haul all sorts of cargo, including helicopters, armored vehicles, and troops. They are the main plane used to airdrop troops and supplies into enemy territory.

# ALPHABET SOUP

The military has a system for naming planes. Letters mean the mission. Numbers identify the design. Letters after numbers tell which part in the series the plane is.

A = Attack
B = Bomber
C = Cargo/Transport
E = Special Electronics
F = Fighter
G = Grounded (for training)
H = Helicopter
J = Special Test

K = Tanker
L = Cold Weather
M = Special Operations
O = Observation
P = Patrol
Q = Unmanned
R = Reconnaissance
S = Anti-submarine
T = Trainer

U = Utility
V = formerly Vertical Landing/now Staff
W = Weather
X = Research/Experimental
Y = Prototype
Z = Planning/ Pre-Development

# HELICOPTERS

Helicopters have some big advantages over airplanes. They take off and land vertically. Plus, they can stay in one spot while in the air and fly close to the ground.

SH-60 Seahawk

The H-60, known as the Black Hawk in the Army, has many versions. The HH-60G Pave Hawk is a search and rescue helicopter for the Air Force. The SH-60 Seahawk performs many Navy missions. The Coast Guard uses the HH-60J Jayhawk for search and rescue missions.

AH-64D Longbow

The AH-64 Apache and AH-64D Longbow are Army attack helicopters.

The U.S. military's largest helicopter is the H-53. The CH-53E is called "Super Stallion." It can carry about 40 Marines.

## CROSSOVER

The AV-8B Harrier II is a fighter jet and bomber. It's also like a helicopter because it can take off vertically and hang in midair. Harriers can take off from ships without being launched like other fighter jets.

# Ships

When a military response is needed, the president asks, "Where are the carriers?" Carriers are like small cities. They even have their own zip codes. About 2,500 airmen join the other 3,000 sailors aboard. It's like having a city that can move around the world and respond to any threat, anywhere.

The catapults on aircraft carriers propel airplanes to 165 miles (266 kilometers) per hour in two seconds! A carrier has four catapults.

The hull is made from steel plates several inches thick.

The hangar deck is below the flight deck. More than 80 aircraft are stored here.

The engine rooms contain nuclear-powered engine systems. They produce more than 280,000 horsepower.

The island houses the bridge and primary flight control, or pri-fly. The captain directs the carrier's actions and movements from the bridge. The Air Boss directs the aircraft from pri-fly.

The top deck is the flight deck. Planes take off and land here for a fast air strike.

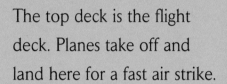

The arresting gear lands a plane in just two seconds. A plane's tailhook grabs a wire stretched across the landing strip. The wire connects to an engine that absorbs the force of the plane as it lands.

Elevators move aircraft from the hangar deck to the flight deck.

Aircraft carriers join other warships in carrier strike groups. The groups might have one or two cruisers, two or three destroyers, a frigate, and a couple of attack submarines.

Cruisers are large warships. The Ticonderoga class is 567 feet (173 meters) long. Its 24 officers and 340 sailors are usually the first at battle.

Destroyers are slightly shorter than cruisers. The Arleigh Burke class destroyers are 505 feet (154 meters) long. They carry about 270 crew members.

Frigates are smaller yet, at about 445 feet (136 meters) long. They have similar weapons to cruisers and destroyers, but frigates defend mainly against enemy submarines.

destroyer

frigate

# BREAKING
# THE ICE

The U.S. Coast Guard uses many ships to defend the country's shores. Cutters are the largest, at 65 feet (19.8 meters) or longer. The 420-foot (128-meter) *HEALY* cutter is the country's newest icebreaker.

cruiser

# SUBMARINES

Sleek, silent submarines are the military's underwater firepower. These underwater wonders run on nuclear power, which is quiet and long-lasting.

The Navy has two main kinds of submarines. Ballistic missile submarines carry nuclear warheads. They represent the United States' ability to launch nuclear weapons even if the mainland United States has been destroyed. Attack submarines carry missiles, torpedoes, and mines to fight enemy subs and ships.

## LIVING ON A SUB

Living in a submarine is like living in a very narrow, windowless three-story building for three months. Attack submarines have a crew of about 140. Only men work on subs. Submariners work for six hours and have 12 hours off. They have 15 square feet (1.4 square meters) of personal space. That includes a place to sleep and store belongings. Luckily, they do get a curtain on their bunk for privacy.

# EQUIPMENT

Submarines have periscopes to see above water. Subs use **sonar** to find enemy ships. Sonar can pick up the sound of a breaking dish or a sailor's squeaky shoes on another sub.

attack submarine

## Fun Fact:

There are four meals served a day on a submarine: breakfast, lunch, dinner, and the midnight snack, called "midrats."

**torpedo** – a missile that travels underwater

**sonar** – a device that uses sound waves to find underwater objects; sonar stands for SOund NAvigation and Ranging.

# LARCs, AAVs, AND LCACs

Crossover vehicles are two vehicles in one. They can float on water and drive on land. All of these crossover vehicles take troops and supplies from ship to shore, and beyond.

The Light Amphibious Resupply Cargo (LARC) vehicle is a half-boat and half-wheeled vehicle. It's 35 feet (10.7 meters) long. The LARC-5 mainly hauls supplies to shore.

The Amphibious Assault Vehicle (AAV) looks like a floating tank. It hauls Marines from ship to shore. But this tracked vehicle can also carry 21 people up to 400 miles (640 kilometers) inland on a full fuel tank.

The Landing Craft Air Cushion, or LCAC, is a **hovercraft** that can travel more than 50 miles (80 kilometers) per hour. LCACs are big vehicles, at 47 feet (14.3 meters) wide and nearly 88 feet (26.8 meters) long. They can carry an Abrams tank or other supplies up to 60 tons (54 metric tons).

**hovercraft** — a vehicle that travels on a cushion of air over both land and water

# UNMANNED VEHICLES

To keep troops out of harm's way, the military is experimenting with vehicles without people inside. The vehicles can explode mines, watch enemy movement, and launch missiles. Meanwhile, the crew operates them by remote from miles away. In the future, you can expect more use of robots in our armed forces.

Pack bot is designed to fit in a soldier's backpack. Soldiers can control its arm remotely to explode bombs and other weapons.

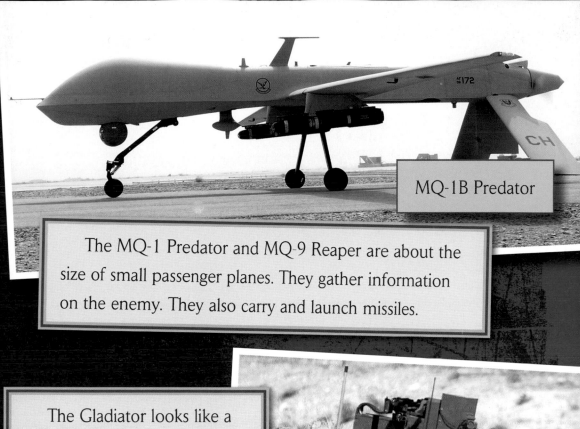

MQ-1B Predator

The MQ-1 Predator and MQ-9 Reaper are about the size of small passenger planes. They gather information on the enemy. They also carry and launch missiles.

The Gladiator looks like a mini tank. It can be mounted with cameras and guns. It also can shoot grenades.

The Raven weighs less than 5 pounds (2.3 kilograms) and can be launched by hand. It gathers information on the enemy.

# GLOSSARY

**hovercraft** (HUHV-ur-kraft) — a vehicle that travels on a cushion of air over both land and water

**infantry** (IN-fuhn-tree) — members of the military trained to fight on land

**Mach** (MAHK) — a unit of measurement for speeds faster than the speed of sound; Mach 2 is twice the speed of sound; the speed of sound is about 760 miles (1,223 kilometers) per hour at sea level.

**nuclear** (NOO-klee-ur) — having to do with the energy created by splitting atoms; nuclear bombs use this energy to cause an explosion; nuclear reactors on subs use this energy as a power source.

**payload** (PAY-lohd) — the total weight of items carried by an airplane

**radar** (RAY-dar) — a device that uses radio waves to track the location of objects

**sonar** (SOH-nar) — a device that uses sound waves to find underwater objects; sonar stands for sound navigation and ranging.

**torpedo** (tor-PEE-doh) — an underwater missile

# Read More

**Fridell, Ron.** *Military Technology.* Cool Science. Minneapolis: Lerner, 2008.

**Graham, Ian.** *Military Vehicles.* Designed for Success. Chicago: Heinemann, 2008.

**Hama, Larry, and Bill Cain.** *Unmanned Aerial Vehicles.* High-Tech Military Weapons. New York: Children's Press, 2007.

**Shuter, Jane.** *War Machines: Military Vehicles Past and Present.* Travel through Time. Portsmouth, Chicago: Raintree, 2004.

# Internet Sites

FactHound offers a safe, fun way to find Internet sites related to this book. All of the sites on FactHound have been researched by our staff.

Here's all you do:

Visit *www.facthound.com*

FactHound will fetch the best sites for you!

# INDEX